Bibliographic information published by the German National Library:

The German National Library lists this publication in the National Bibliography; detailed bibliographic data are available on the Internet at http://dnb.dnb.de .

Imprint:

Copyright © 2006 GRIN Verlag
Print and binding: Books on Demand GmbH, Norderstedt Germany
ISBN: 9783668800175

This book at GRIN:

https://www.grin.com/document/125887

Eleonora Reis

Religion in Flannery O'Connor's "A Good Man is Hard to Find"

GRIN Verlag

GRIN - Your knowledge has value

Since its foundation in 1998, GRIN has specialized in publishing academic texts by students, college teachers and other academics as e-book and printed book. The website www.grin.com is an ideal platform for presenting term papers, final papers, scientific essays, dissertations and specialist books.

Katholische Universität Eichstätt-Ingolstadt

Institut für Anglistik und Amerikanistik

Proseminar: „Modern American Short Stories"

Summer Semester 2005

Religion in Flannery O`Connor`s

"A Good Man Is Hard to Find"

Eleonora Reis

Lehramt Grundschule

4. Semester

Table of Contents:

1. Introduction

At first sight "A Good Man Is Hard to Find" by Flannery O`Connor just appears like a grotesque story because it begins with a happy family trip and ends with a conversation about Jesus and six murders. But if the story is read under the aspect of religion, it has indeed got a deeper meaning. The fact that the author herself was a very religious woman, as will be obvious from her biography, and that religion appears in all of her works, shows that this short story can only be interpreted with the focus on religion.

2. Main Part

2.1   Flannery O`Connor`s Biography

To know about the life of Flannery O`Connor is important to understand her work. O`Connor`s life was characterized by her devotion to Roman Catholic faith and her Southern uprising, which is reflected in her stories. Therefore, her biography is important for the interpretation of *A Good Man Is Hard To Find*.

O`Connor was born on 25 March 1925 in Savannah, Georgia. She was an only child in a middle class Southern Catholic family, whose father was a real estate broker.[1]

Her education to Roman Catholic faith began early as her first school years, which fell into the time of the Depression, took place in the Cathedral of St. John the Baptist, which was located near the house of her parents.[2] Already at the age of six years, she showed a talent for writing and illustrating her own stories. In 1938, her father was diagnosed with lupus erythematosus and therefore the family moved to Milledgeville, Georgia, in the same year. Milledgeville was her mother`s birthplace and more Protestant and tranquil than Savannah. At High School, O`Connor wrote satirical articles and drew illustrations for the school paper. At that time, she was very interested in the genre of satire, but later she found that this genre`s limits were too narrow for her talent and religious concerns.[3] In 1941, O´Connor`s father died of his disease and therefore she and her mother moved to her mother`s family farm *Andalusia*, which is a few miles outside Milledgeville. O`Connor studied at the Georgia State College for Women and in 1945, she graduated with a major in

---

1   Cf. Evan Goodwin, *Little blue light - Flannery O`Connor*. 12 May 2003.
         11.09.05 <http://www.littlebluelight.com/lblphp/intro.php?ikey=20> 1.

2   Cf. Margaret Earley Whitt, *Understanding Flannery O`Connor* (Columbia:
         University of South Carolina Press, 1995) 6.

3   Cf. Goodwin 1.

social science.[4] During her college time, she was editor of the school newspaper and the literary journal. Then she moved to New York City and later to the Connecticut farmhouse of Robert and Sally Fitzgerald, who were friends of hers from New York, and lived there for only a few months. During that time, she started working on her first novel *Wise Blood*.

At the age of 25, she showed first signs of lupus, the disease that had killed her father in 1941.[5] Lupus erythematosus is an autoimmune disease, that infests the skin, inner organs, the kidney and brain and leads inevitably to death.[6]

O`Connor thought she had only three more years to live, like her father did after he had showed the first symptoms, but in fact she lived on for 14 more years. But instead of resigning over her fate, she saw it as an opportunity to refine her art of writing. She returned to the South and to *Andalusia*, where her mother could care for her.[7] She spent the rest of her life writing, visiting friends and reading.[8]

Her first novel *Wise Blood* was published in 1952, but the reviews were bad because they branded it as only grotesque and nihilistic. Therefore, O`Connor immediately began working on her second novel *The Violent Bear It Away*. Then she turned to writing short stories, which were honoured with three O. Henry Awards.[9] Her short fiction shows autobiographical influences because *The Life You Save May Be Your Own*, *Good Country People*, *A Circle in the Fire* and other stories contain a woman, who lives on a farm with her solitary daughter.[10] Although O`Connor could only walk on crutches from 1955 on, she travelled to Lourdes and to Rome and lectured at several colleges. In 1960, *The Violent Bear It Away* was published, but again the reviews were bad as the novel was labelled anti-Catholic and therefore was misunderstood. O`Connor died on 3 August 1964 at her home in Milledgeville.[11]

---

4   Cf. Whitt 6-7.

5   Cf. Goodwin 2.

6   Cf. Theodor von Keudell, *Das Große Lexikon der Modernen Medizin* (Bergisch Gladbach: Lingen Verlag, 1994) 259-60.

7   Cf. Goodwin 2.

8   Cf. Whitt 7.

9   Cf. Goodwin 2.

10   Cf. Whitt 7.

11   Cf. Goodwin 3.

2.2 Summary of the Short Story:

The story begins with a seemingly happy family trip from Atlanta to Florida. The participants of the trip are Bailey, who is the father of the family, his wife, his children, who are called June Star and John Wesley, their baby and the grandmother, who is Bailey's mother.

Before the trip, the grandmother tries to persuade Bailey rather to go to Tennessee than to Florida because she wants to visit some of her friends there. She warns him that a convict called "The Misfit" has escaped from the Federal Penitentiary and is on his way toward Florida. In her opinion, it would be irresponsible to go the same direction. Neither Bailey, nor his wife react to what the grandmother says, only June Star and John Wesley talk to her in a rude way and imply that they would rather want the grandmother to stay at home.

The following day, the grandmother hides her cat, Pitty Sing, in the car, as she knows for sure that Bailey doesn't want to take the cat with him on the journey. The grandmother's fear is that the cat might unintentionally turn on one of the gas burners and suffocate. During the drive, the grandmother comments on the landscape, but she is being ignored by the rest of the family as the children are reading comic books, their mother is sleeping and Bailey is driving without talking. Only June Star and John Wesley react to the grandmother's comments and stories, but again in a rude and disrespectful way.

Then they have a break for a snack at *The Tower*, which is a filling station and dance hall at the same time. The grandmother talks to the owner of *The Tower*, who is called Red Sammy Butts, about the Misfit and his possible prescence in their region. When they continue their journey, the grandmother remembers an old mansion with a plantation near Toombsboro, that she has once visited in her youth. As she thinks this mansion to be in the neighbourhood and as she knows exactly that Bailey won't be willing to look at an old house, she invents a secret panel, in which some silver is hidden, in order to make the children want to look at the house. The grandmother's plan is successful and the children start to whine until Bailey finally agrees to go to the mansion and follows the grandmother's description of the way. Suddenly, the grandmother remembers that the plantation, that they are looking for, is not in Georgia, where they are located, but in Tennessee. Consequently, the grandmother is so startled, that she hits the basket with her foot, where she has hidden Pitty Sing before. As a result, the cat springs onto Bailey and the car turns over. Just then, a car arrives with three men in it, of whom everybody has a gun. One of them is recognized by the grandmother as The Misfit and this moment is virtually the death sentence for the whole family. The Misfit and the grandmother get along very well with each other and while they are talking about his parents, being in prison, praying and Jesus, his mates, Hiram and Bobby Lee, kill first Bailey and John Wesley and then his wife, the baby and June Star in the woods. Finally, The Misfit shoots the grandmother, after she has tried to touch him on the shoulder.

2.3   Character Analysis

2.3.1   Bailey

Bailey is ignorant towards his mother because she is talking to him and even "rattling the newspaper at his bald head"[12], but nevertheless he doesn`t look up to her or even answer her. In the beginning, Bailey appears like the strong leader of the family, who has everybody and everything under his control: the grandmother may not take Pitty Sing with her because Bailey doesn`t "like to arrive at a motel with a cat" (118) and he is the one, who decides whether or not the family is going to look at the house with the secret panel. On the other side, he is very taciturn as he hardly says anything or "he only glare[s] at her" (121) when the grandmother asks him to dance. He is also quite irritable and nervous because when his children wail for visiting the mansion, "[h]is jaw [is] as rigid as a horseshoe" (123). Finally, he explodes and tells his family three times to shut up. Therefore, he makes a very rude and cold-hearted impression. Actually, this is the first time in the story that Bailey becomes active and really says something.

Bailey`s reiterations are striking as he first tells his family repeatedly to shut up, then he explains to them twice that "[t]his is the one and only time" (124) he is going to stop the car and finally, when he is confronted with death through the Misfit, he can only repeat that "[they]`re in a terrible predicament" (128). Probably Bailey`s reiterations are the reason for why the author has equipped him with "bright blue parrots" (125) on his shirt. His reiterations show that Bailey has a fixed behaviour-pattern: as soon as something disturbs him or a problem appears, he repeats his usual sentences over and over again, trying to restore his order and to regain control.

When the family meets the Misfit, Bailey is the only one of them who sees the danger of their situation and he is right when he says that "[n]obody realizes what this is" (128). He tries to gain control over the situation and tells his family to "let [him] handle this" (ibid.). Thus, he wants to break out of his passivity and and significantly is "squatting in the

---

12   Flannery O`Connor, *The Complete Stories* (New York: Farrar, Straus and Giroux, 1974) 117. All

   parenthetical references follow this edition.

position of a runner about to sprint forward" (ibid.), but he fails as "he remain[s] perfectly still" (ibid.).

In the course of events, Bailey changes from the strong leader of the family to a weak and broken man because "his voice crack[s]" (ibid.) and he has to "support himself against a […] pine trunk" (ibid.). When he finally faces death, he expresses his first nice words toward the grandmother as he calls her "Mama" (ibid.).

2.3.2   The Children`s Mother

Like the grandmother, the mother has got no real name, but is always referred to as "the children`s mother". Her outward appearance is described in a grotesque way as her "face [is] as broad and innocent as a cabbage" (117) and she wears "a green head-kerchief that [has] two points on the top like a rabbit`s ears" (ibid.). According to her looks, the mother stands in sharp contrast to the grandmother because whereas the grandmother attaches great importance to a lady-like dress-code, the mother "still [has] on slacks and […] a green kerchief" (118) on the second day.

Like Bailey, his wife is also ignoring the grandmother because when the grandmother tries to persuade them to go to east Tennessee, "[t]he children`s mother [doesn`t] seem to hear her" (117) and during the drive, the mother doesn`t listen or react to the grandmother`s comments on the passing landscape, but she "[has] gone back to sleep" (119).

What is striking about the mother, is her passivity: she only expresses three sentences in the whole story. She also doesn`t seem to have her own will because when the grandmother wants to hold the baby, "the children`s mother passe[s] him over the front seat to her" (119) and when June Star wants to tap, "the children`s mother put[s] in another dime" (121). She also doesn`t reprove her children when firstly John Wesley is disrespectful toward his grandmother by calling Tennessee "a hillbilly dumping ground" (119) and secondly when June Star is rude to Red Sammy`s wife by telling her that she "wouldn`t live in a broken-down place like this for a million bucks" (121). Anyway, it is not the mother, but the grandmother, who educates the children as she disciplines June Star when she is rude and she is the one, who orders the chilrden not to throw the garbage out of the window.

The mother becomes active only two times in the story. The first time is when she orders that "[they]`ll all stay in the car" (124) and the second time is when she shouts at the Misfit where his henchmen are taking her husband. But when the Misfit doesn`t react to her question, she falls back into her passivity and only replies "[y]es, thank you" (131), when he asks her to join Bailey in the woods.

2.3.3   June Star and John Wesley

Although the children are often rude and disrespectful, they are at the same time very honest and direct. As the grandmother doesn`t want to go to Florida, it is legitimate when John Wesley asks her "why dontcha stay at home?" (117). But in spite of their rudeness, the children are the only ones of the family who respond to the grandmother. What is remarkable about June Star is that she is too grown up for her young age. She is very proud and has already got fixed principles because she knows for sure that "she wouldn`t marry a man that just brought her a watermelon on Saturday" (120). Even when she is confronted with three armed strangers, she asks them fearlessly and rude "What are you telling US what to do for?" (127). Her fearlessness and pride don`t even leave her when she faces death because still then she tells her killer that " [h]e reminds [her] of a pig" (131). John Wesley also proves his courage when he asks the Misfit "What you got that gun for?" (126). But when he faces death, he expresses feelings toward his father for the first time as he "[catches] hold of his father`s hand" (128).

But there are also some grotesque features about the children. They are quite sensation-seeking when they scream three times "We`ve had an ACCIDENT!" (125, 126) after the car has turned over, and the fact that they scream it with "delight" (125) makes the situation even more absurd. Furthermore, June Star makes a cold-hearted and brutal impression when she says disappointedly that "nobody`s killed" (ibid.) after she has discovered that the grandmother is still alive. The children also appear involiable as everybody has to recover after the accident "except the children" (ibid.). The monkey outside *The Tower* feels this cold-heartedness and fearlessness of the two children and therefore "[gets] on the highest limb as soon as he [sees] the children [...] run toward him" (121).

2.3.4   The Grandmother

Like the children`s mother, the grandmother does`t have a personal name because she actually isn`t an individual person but she conforms to the general stereotype of a grandmother: she talks carelessly all day long and tells stories about her time when "[p]eople [still] did right" (119). She seems to still live in the past because she tells the children stories about the time when she was "a maiden lady" (120) and during The Tennessee Waltz, "[s]he sway[s] her head from side to side and pretend[s] she [is] dancing in her chair" (121). But she doesn't talk realistically about the old times, instead she embellishes the past in her memory as with the mansion she once visited that had "six white columns across the front" (123) and "an avenue of oaks leading up to it" (ibid.). The grandmother also dresses in the Old Southern style with "white cotton gloves" (118) and "a navy blue straw sailor hat" (ibid.). She attaches great importance to small details like the "bunch of white violets on the brim [of her hat]" (118) or the "purple spray of cloth violets" (ibid.), that she has pinned at her neckline. Thus, it is very important for her to look like a lady, but on the other side, she behaves like a racist when she talks about a "pickaninny" (119) and "[l]ittle niggers" (ibid.) and therefore she appears not at all lady-like. The grandmother is a very extrovert person in contrast to her son and his wife, as she talks about the landscape during the trip, she tells the children stories and is "very dramatic" (120). She cares for her cat and educates the children, and she talks to strangers like Red Sammy and the Misfit in an intimate way. She also talks to Bailey and his wife although they are not answering her. Even the baby seems to ignore her and to be bored by her talking because he only occasionally gives her "a faraway smile" (119).

The grandmother is quite naïve and makes a hasty judgement when she calls Red Sammy a "good man" (122) because she watches him treating his wife very bad as he doesn`t help her when she carries five plates with food on her own and he interrupts her in the middle of a sentence and tells her to hurry up with the family`s drinks (cf. 122). She also calls the Misfit a good man even though she doesn`t know him at all. He has only said ten sentences when the grandmother judges him as good and thus, this can`t be a carefully thought out judgement.

The fact that the grandmother`s thinking is egocentric comes out when she tells the Misfit "I recognized you at once" (127) and as a consequence signs the death-sentence of the whole family as she doesn`t think of the consequences of what she says. Her selfishness is also shown when she says "You wouldn`t shoot a lady, would you?" (ibid.). Thus, the first thing that she thinks of, after she has realized that they all will have to die, is her own life and not the lives of the whole family. In order to get her will, she even doesn`t refrain from lying as she invents a secret panel so that the children desparately want to look at the mansion she has remembered. Even shortly before her son is shot, the grandmother only thinks about herself and her look as she "reache[s] up to adjust her hat brim" (128). But then she seems to lose interest in outward appearance as "she let[s] [the hat] fall on the ground" (ibid.). But this impression is destroyed when she offers the murderer of her own son "an extra shirt in [Bailey's] suitcase" (129), so that the Misfit doesn't have to stand with a bare chest before the ladies.

What is most striking about the grandmother's talking in the second half of the story, are her permanent reiterations: Six times she asks the Misfit to pray (cf. 129, 130, 132), she assures him three times that she knows he's "a good man" (127, 128) and twice that he is not "common" (127, 128). She tells him three times not to "shoot a lady" (127, 132) and twice that he must "come from nice people" (127, 132). The reason for the grandmother's behaviour is that she is very desparate and does everything she can to save her life. She repeats her statements about Jesus and praying over and over again because this is what she has grown up with and in her opinion fits to every situation. But the grandmother's speech is contradictory as on the one hand she affirms the Misfit "If you would pray, […] Jesus would help you." (130) and appears like a deeply religious woman, but on the other hand she doubts Jesus'actions as she proves with her statement that "[m]aybe He didn't raise the dead" (132). As a consequence, she cannot seem trustworthy in the Misfit's eyes and this is also shown in the way she is saying "Jesus" because "it sound[s] as if she might be cursing" (131).

2.3.5 The Misfit

The Misfit's language shows a strong Southern accent and a lot of grammar and spelling mistakes. His Southern accent is perceptible in expressions like "Yes'm" (127), "Nome" (128) and "mam" (127). The Misfit's sentence construction is very simple, but he makes severe grammar mistakes like "he don't mean" (ibid.), "it never come" (130) and "I forget what I done" (ibid.). He uses colloquial speech because he says "I ain't recalled" (ibid.) or "I ain't a good man" (128) and he uses the simplification "head-doctor" (130) instead of "psychiatrist". The Misfit's colloquial speech and his severe spelling mistakes like "to ast" (128), "you […] reckernized me" (127) or "Thow me that shirt" (130) prove that he had very little schooling. He also uses doublings quite often like "you all had you a little spill" (126), "Nobody had nothing" (130) or "It wasn't no mistake" (ibid.).

But in spite of the mistakes in his speech, the Misfit shows quite good manners as he calls the children's mother and the grandmother a "lady" (126-132) and he apologizes for not "hav[ing] on a shirt before [the] ladies" (129). Because of his good manners and his Southern accent, the Misfit seems familiar to the grandmother and therefore she believes him to be a good man at once.

In the story, the Misfit is often described as vulnerable and sensitive because "his ankles [are] red and thin" (126) and the grandmother notices "how thin his shoulder blades" (129) are. Furthermore, "[t]he Misfit`s eyes [are] red-rimmed and pale and defenseless-looking" (132- 133), after he has killed the grandmother. He also appears quite sympathetic when he tries to comfort the grandmother by telling her not to "get upset [because] [s]ometimes a man says things he do[es]`t mean" (127). But the Misfit`s feelings prove to be fake and superficial because it is said that "he *seem*[s] [my emphases] to be embarrassed" (ibid.) and he looks "*as if* [my emphases] he were embarrassed" (129). Furthermore, his face looks "*as if* [my emphases] he were going to cry" (132) and "[h]is voice *seem*[s] [my emphases] about to crack" (ibid.). As a consequence, the narrator implies that the Misfit`s feelings are only fake and not real. And indeed, the Misfit`s insincerity proves when he tries to make a fool of Bailey by telling him that his henchmen only "want to as[k] [him] something" (128), although it is clear that they are going to shoot him. The Misfit also tells the grandmother that they "borrowed [their clothes] from some folks [they] met" (129), although they obviously stole them.

The grandmother seems to be the only person, whom the Misfit feels connected to because she is the only one of the whole family, whom he responds and really talks to. Therefore, he doesn`t answer when John Wesley asks him what he is going to do with his gun (cf. 126) or when June Star asks him why he`s giving them orders (cf. 127) or when Bailey`s wife wants to know where they are taking her husband (cf. 129).

2.4   Religion in "A Good Man Is Hard to Find"

2.4.1   The Jesus-Question

In the grandmother`s life, Jesus has got no importance, although she is talking about religion very much. But for the Misfit, Jesus plays a very important role because if he really could raise the dead,

> then it`s nothing for you to do but throw away everything and follow Him, and if He didn`t, then it`s nothing for you to do but enjoy the few minutes you got left the best way you can – by killing somebody or burning down his house or doing some other meanness to him (132).

In contrast to the grandmother, the Misfit is thinking very much about Jesus and his words have very deep meaning for him. On the one hand, the Misfit seems to truly believe in Christ as he claims that "Jesus was the only One that ever raised the dead" (132), but on the other hand he wonders if this really is true as he objects "I wasn`t there so I can`t say He didn`t" (ibid.). For the Misfit, Jesus mixed up the whole world order though his actions and he is the only one responsible for the Misfit`s confusion because he "th[r]own everything off balance" (131, 132). In the Misfit`s opinion, Jesus "shouldn`t have done it" (132) because he couldn`t be there to see for himself and thus to have evidence, but he is sure that "if [he] had of been there [he] would of known [...] and [he] wouldn`t be like [he is] now" (ibid.). Consequently, the Misfit`s thinking is very extreme as for him, there is no middle between the total commitment of faith and the total commitment of disbelief. Thus, the Misfit constructs his own logic and he lets his whole life depend on something that happened long ago in the past.

The Misfit suffers very much from the fact that he doesn`t know for sure whether or not Jesus was God because he doesn´t have any proof. Marshall Bruce Gentry is right when he claims that, for the Misfit, Jesus has not thrown everything off balance bacause he could raise the dead, but because of "Christ`s freedom from any fixed, reliable, deadening text."[13] On the one hand, the Misfit struggles with the Jesus-question, but on the other hand, he appears very self-righteous when he says that "[n]obody [has] nothing [he] want[s]" (130) and that he doesn`t want anybody`s help because "[he is] doing all right by [him]self" (ibid.).

There are several references in the text to "the cloudless sky" (130,132). According to Kathleen Feeley, sun and clouds are biblical symbols for divinity and grace. As a result, the fact that "[t]here [is] not a cloud in the sky nor any sun" (131), suggests that divinity and grace are not present in the Misfit`s life and this is indeed true as he rejects Jesus and his grace.[14] The reason for the Misfit not being able to have faith, is that he cannot believe in something that he hasn`t seen with his own eyes and that he cannot explain logically. Appropriately, the Misfit`s father already said that his son always "has to know why it is" (129). Therefore, the Misfit cannot develop faith and is excluded from spirituality. In

---

13   Marshall Bruce Gentry, *Flannery O`Connor`s Religion of the Grotesque* (Jackson: University Press of Mississippi, 1986) 111.

14   Cf. Kathleen Feeley, *Flannery O`Connor: Voice of the Peacock.* (New York: Fordham University Press, 1982) 74.

contrast to the Misfit, the grandmother looks upon the world the way she wants to see it. This is for example shown in her statement that "Europe [is] entirely to blame for the way things [are] now" (122). But the Misfit approaches reality truly. This is shown when he corrects the grandmother that the car didn`t turn over twice, but "[o]nce[…] [because they have] seen it happen" (126).

2.4.2   The Misfit`s Sense of Injustice and the Amnesia of His Crimes

The Misfit seems to suffer from amnesia of his crimes because when he got sent to prison, he "set there and set there, trying to remember what it was [he had] done and [he] ain`t recalled it to this day" (130). But there is a contradiction in his speech because although he "never was a bad boy that [he] remember[s] of" (ibid.), he is sure that "[i]t wasn`t no mistake" (ibid.), when the grandmother suggests that they maybe took him to prison by mistake.

The Misfit claims that the prison-psychiatrist told him that he has killed his father, but he "know[s] that for a lie" (130). As a result, the Misfit either repressed the patricide until he completely forgot about it or, according to Marshall Bruce Gentry, he misunderstood the psychiatrist as he told the Misfit that "he needs to desecrate the image of his father" because "he has an Oedipus complex"[15], but the Misfit understood that he shall have killed his father. But from the text only it is not clear whether or not he committed the murder of his father.

For the Misfit, "the crime [doesn`t] matter […] because sooner or later you`re going to forget what it was you [have] done and just be punished for it" (130). The Misfit feels that he is being treated unjustly because he doesn`t consider punishment as the logical consequence of his crimes. And because he has got no memory of his crimes, he can`t understand what he is actually being punished for. As a result, the Misfit has decided to "sign everything [he does] and keep a copy of it" (131). By signing his acts himself, the Misfit expects to gain evidence in order "to prove [he] ain`t been treated right" (ibid.) because then he "can hold up the crime to the punishment and see do they match" (ibid.).

The Misfit`s explanation for why he is actually called "Misfit" can be interpreted in two ways: he says he "can`t make what all [he has] done wrong fit what all [he has] gone through in punishment" (131). Either he feels that he has done very little, but is being

---

15   Gentry 109.

13

punished a heap because he cannot remember what he actually has done, or he believes that he has been punished very little, although he has committed a lot of crimes. Both interpretations seem reasonably, but what can be said in favour of the second one, is the fact that at the very moment, when Bailey`s wife, the baby and June Star are being shot in the woods, the Misfit asks the grandmother if "it seem[s] right to [her] [...] that one is punished a heap and another ain`t punished at all" (ibid.). And because the Misfit has escaped from prison, he is consequently the one, who isn`t punished at all at that point of time.

2.4.3 The Grandmother`s Adoption of the Misfit and Her "Moment of Grace"

The grandmother seems to more and more accept the Misfit as a son because first she calls " ́Bailey Boy!` [...] but she found she [is] looking at The Misfit" (128). After that she offers him "an extra shirt in [her son`s] suitcase" (129), then the Misfit really puts on Bailey`s shirt and finally, the grandmother even calls him "one of [her] own children" (132). But simultaneously with her attempt to adopt him, the grandmother tries to gain parental authority over the Misfit because she is significantly "standing up looking down on him" (129) and "The Misfit [is] squatting on the ground in front of her" (128). One reading of the Misfit killing the grandmother is that he rejects being subjugated by her."[16]

The story could be read like the grandmother is only in a state of shock because she realizes that she will have to die and therefore, she calls the Misfit "one of her babies" (132) just out of confusion. But from the author`s biography, it is obvious that O`Connor was very religious and for that reason, the story has to have a deeper meaning.

At first, the grandmother indeed seems to be confused as she is "not knowing what she [is] saying and feeling [...] dizzy" (132), but then her "head clear[s] for an instant" (ibid.) and she recognizes the Misfit as "one of [her] children" (ibid.). At that moment, she doen`t seem to be confused at all, but what she says is rather a realization. The grandmother accepts the Misfit as her son because she recognizes his suffering and his fighting with the Jesus-question and not because she believes to save her life by her talking as she has done before. Through the whole story, the grandmother tried to behave like a lady and was very egocentric and selfish, but at that moment, for the first time, she thinks about someone other than herself. Thus, the grandmother`s alienation has been ended and she has been

---

16   Cf. Gentry 35.

returned to reality.[17] Althogh the Misfit has just killed her whole family, the grandmother accepts the Misfit in an act of selfless love and such love is only possible through God`s mercy. Therefore, her illumination is a sign for the grandmother`s moment of grace.[18]

The Misfit`s statement that "[s]he would of been a good woman [...], if it had been somebody there to shoot her every minute of her life" (133) shows that he realizes, that only when the grandmother is facing death through the Misfit`s violence, she can be kept aware. Then she is not alienated any more, but turns from a "lady" to a "good woman".[19] His henchman Bobby Lee first believes he is joking, but the Misfit is serious and therefore tells Bobby Lee to "[s]hut up" (ibid.). The grandmother`s enlightment is also visible from both her face and her body as "her legs [are] crossed under her like a child`s and her face is smiling up at the cloudless sky" (132). Her expression suggests that she returns to a childlike and innocent state and this has indeed been her wish as, during her lifetime, she has always been talking and dreaming of "the old times".[20]

But the Misfit cannot accept the grandmother`s love and foregiveness, as well as he cannot accept Jesus` foregiveness, and therefore he kills her in another rejection of Jesus.[21]

When the grandmother touches the Misfit, he "[springs] back as if a snake [has] bitten him and [shoots] her three times through the chest" (132). In the Bible, the snake symbolyses the devil and the number three symbolyses the Christian Trinity and therefore goodness. Margaret Early Whitt draws the conclusion that "In an allegorical reading, the devil is destroyed by Christ`s goodness."[22] This may seem grotesque at first sight because in this reading, the grandmother, who is full of love, stands for the devil and the Misfit, who is full of meanness, stands for goodness. But is must be considered that from the Misfit`s point of view, the grandmother`s gesture is perceived as the Snake`s temptation because, like Jesus, she throws everything off balance, and therefore he considers her shooting as good and as the reestablishment of his own order.[23]

---

17   Cf. Feeley 73.

18   Cf. David Eggenschwiler, *The Christian Humanism of Flannery O`Connor.* (Detroit: Wayne State University Press, 1972) 92.

19   Cf. Feeley 73. Gentry 112.

20   Cf. Miles Orvell, *Invisible Parade: The Fiction of Flannery O`Connor* (Philadelphia: Temple University Press, 1972) 132. Gentry 35.

21   Cf. Eggenschwiler 92.

22   Whitt 48.

23   Cf. Orvell 133.

Although the Misfit rejects the grandmother, he makes the impression as if her death has brought a change for him because, for the first time in the story, "he put[s] his gun down on the ground and [takes] off his glasses" (132) af if he were disarmed. He also looks different as his eyes are "red-rimmed and pale and defenseless-looking" (132-133). Finally, the change in his attitude is obvious when he realizes that "[i]t`s no real pleasure in life" (133) because now he sees that meanness is not a pleasure, whereas before he has explained to the grandmother that you should seek meanness as a pleasure.[24] This mouvement for the Misfit is confirmed though O`Connor`s own comment as " ´the old lady`s gesture, like the mustard-seed, will grow to be a great crow-filled tree in the Misfit`s heart, and will be enough of a pain to him there to turn him into the prophet he was meant to become` ".[25]

2.5 The Author`s Style

2.5.1 Foreshadowings

There are many foreshadowings in the text. By means of these, the narrator implies that there will be death at the end of the story. First the grandmother draws Bailey`s attention to a newspaper article about the Misfit and wants him to read "what it says he did to these people" (117). Then the narrator explains that the reason for the grandmother paying so much attention to her outward appearance is that "[i]n case of an accident, anyone seeing her dead on the highway would know at once that she was a lady" (118). Later it is told that "[t]hey passed [...] five or six graves" (119) and thus, the six murders of the family members are predicted. The narrator also describes the Misfit`s car appropriately as a "hearse-like automobile" (126). From the moment on that the family turns onto the dirt road toward the old masion, the atmosphere in the story becomes dark and sinister. The road is described with "sudden washes", "sharp curves" and "dangerous embankments" (124). In this way, the narrator implies that the family is driving toward disaster. Significantly, he uses dark and strong colours to describe the dangerous situation for the family: he talks of "pink dust", "blue tops of trees" and "a red depression" (124).

2.5.2 Symbolism

Apart from the biblical symbols, that have already been mentioned above, there is the forest, which symbolises danger and ultimately death. When the family turns onto the dirt

---

24   Cf. Whitt 48.

25   Orvell 134.

road, they suddenly find themselves in an area described with "trees for miles around" (124). Furthermore, the family is being observed by "dust-coated trees looking down on them" (ibid.). Before the Misfit arrives at the scene of the car accident, the danger for the family increases and significantly, "there [are] more woods, tall and dark and deep" (125). Shortly before the grandmother tells the Misfit to have recognized him, "the line of woods gape[s] like a dark open mouth" (127) and the reader gets the impression as if the family is about to be swallowed by disaster. Finally, the family members are lead into the woods by the Misfit`s henchmen toward "the dark edge" (128), where death is waiting for them.

2.5.3   Irony, Humour and the Grotesque

There is much irony in the text, especially in the description of the grandmother as the narrator describes her lady-like appearance very detailed and also exaggerated (cf. 118). Irony is also visible when it is said of the grandmother that "[w]hen she [tells] a story, she roll[s] her eyes and wave[s] her head and [is] very dramatic" (120). Even the beginning of the story is ironical because first the grandmother says that she "wouldn`t take [her] children in any direction with a criminal like that aloose in it" (117), but she exactly does this later as she forces the family to make a detour from their originally planned route. But there is also open mockery of the grandmother in the text as the narrator calls her "a parched old turkey hen crying for water" (132). The story also contains some humour, for example when the Misfit tells the grandmother that "there never was a body that g[a]ve the undertaker a tip"(132) after she has offered him all the money she has got. Apart from the description of the mother`s head and the grandmother`s suitcase, the mother`s response "[y]es, thank you" (131) also makes a grotesque impression on the reader as the Misfit has asked her before to join her dead husband in the woods. In general, the story is quite grotesque as it begins like a seemingly funny family trip and ends with the grandmother and a murderer talking about Jesus.

2.5.4   Point of View and Narrator

In the first half of the story, the omnicient narrator appears to be vicious because the family is described in a negative way: the grandmother is annoying Bailey and his wife because she`d rather go to Tennessee that to Florida, in response they are ignoring the grandmother and the children are rude and disrespectful. The narrator also portrays the family members as grotesque because of the mother`s head resembling "a cabbage" with "rabbit`s ears" (117) and the grandmother`s valise looking "like the head of a hippopotamus" (118). The fact that the narrator is quite malicious is also apparent from the foreshadowings. Thus, the narrator implies that the story leads inevitably to death.[26] The narrator also tries to make the reader believe that the deaths of the whole family are the grandmother`s fault: first the grandmother takes the cat, who will later be the reason for the car accident, with her, although Bailey doesn`t permit it. Then the family has got to make a detour because the grandmother desparately wants to see the old mansion that she remembers, which leads them in the very direction of the Misfit. And finally, she tells the Misfit to have recognized him, which makes the murders of the family members quite sure to happen. The first part of the story until the moment when the Misfit enters the scene, is told from the grandmother`s point of view because she is in the center of attention. The story even begins with the grandmother`s view of the trip as the very first sentence is that "[the grandmother] didn`t want to go to Florida" (117). The grandmother`s point of view also becomes obvious when it is said that "[s]he didn`t intend for the cat to be left alone in the house for three days because he would miss her too much and she was afraid he might brush against one of the gas burners and accidentally aphyxiate himself" (118). These are the grandmother`s personal reasons to take the cat with her. But the second half of the story is told from the Misfit`s point of view. This is shown most clearly from the fact that the grandmother`s gesture is perceived by him as the Snake`s temptation and his own act of shooting as good.[27] But not only the point of view changes, the omnicient narrator also loses his viciousness and becomes more objective as he focuses the conversation between the grandmother and the Misfit and not the murders of the family members.

3. Conclusion

It has been proved that if religion and not the murders are in the reader`s focus of attention, only then he can learn the true meaning of the story. This approach is also demanded by the author as she wants the reader to " ´be on the lookout for such things as the action of grace in the Grandmother`s soul, and not for the dead bodies` ".[28]

---

26   Cf. Gentry 32.

27   Cf. Orvell 133.

28   Gentry 36.

4. Bibliography

Primary Sources:

- O`Connor, Flannery. *The Complete Stories.* 8th ed. New York: Farrar, Straus and Giroux, 1974.

Secondary Sources:

- Eggenschwiler, David. *The Christian Humanism of Flannery O`Connor.* Detroit: Wayne State University Press, 1972.

- Feeley, Kathleen. *Flannery O`Connor: Voice of the Peacock.* New York: Fordham University Press, 1982.

- Gentry, Marshall Bruce. *Flannery O`Connor`s Religion of the Grotesque.* Jackson: University Press of Mississippi, 1986.

- Goodwin, Evan. *Little blue light - Flannery O`Connor.* 12 May 2003. 11.09.05. <http://www.littlebluelight.com/lblphp/intro.php?ikey=20>.

- von Keudell, Theodor. *Das große Lexikon der modernen Medizin.* Bergisch Gladbach: Lingen Verlag, 1994.

- Orvell, Miles. *Invisible Parade: The Fiction of Flannery O`Connor.* Philadelphia: Temple University Press, 1972.

- Whitt, Margaret Earley. *Understanding Flannery O`Connor.* Columbia: University of South Carolina Press, 1995.